I0484775

Financial Management

:: Author ::

Hetal Parmar

(M.COM., M.Phil., SLET)

PUBLISHED BY

**The New Era International Publishing House
HQ. At & Po. Chaveli., Ta- Chansma,
Dist- Patan, North Gujarat, India, Asia.
www.iphouseindia.com**

Financial Management

First Publication: 1ST MARCH, 2015

Copyright: Author
(c) Hetal Parmar

ISBN:- 978-15-08949-71-8

Price: Rs.750/- INDIA
    $ 15 OUTSIDE INDIA

PUBLISHED BY

The New Era International Publishing House
HQ. At & Po. Chaveli., Ta- Chansma,
Dist- Patan, North Gujarat, India, Asia.
www.iphouseindia.com

Chapter 01

Introduction to Financial Management

INTRODUCTION

Business concern needs finance to meet their requirements in the economic world. Any kind of business activity depends on the finance. Hence, it is called as lifeblood of business organization. Whether the business concerns are big or small, they need finance to fulfil their business activities.

In the modern world, all the activities are concerned with the economic activities and very particular to earning profit through any venture or activities. The entire business activities are directly related with making profit. (According to the economics concept of factors of production, rent given to landlord, wage given to labour, interest given to capital and profit given to shareholders or proprietors), a business concern needs finance to meet all the requirements. Hence finance may be called as capital, investment, fund etc., but each term is having different meanings and unique characters. Increasing the profit is the main aim of any kind of economic activity.

MEANING OF FINANCE

Finance may be defined as the art and science of managing money. It includes financial service and financial instruments. Finance also is referred as the provision of money at the time when it is needed. Finance function is the procurement of funds and their effective utilization in business concerns.

The concept of finance includes capital, funds, money, and amount. But each word is having unique meaning. Studying and understanding the concept of finance become an important part of the business concern.

DEFINITION OF FINANCE

According to **Khan and Jain,** "Finance is the art and science of managing money".

According to **Oxford dictionary**, the word 'finance' connotes 'management of money'.

Webster's Ninth New Collegiate Dictionary defines finance as "the Science on study of the management of funds' and the management of fund as the system that includes the circulation of money, the granting of credit, the making of investments, and the provision of banking facilities.

DEFINITION OF BUSINESS FINANCE

According to the **Wheeler,** "Business finance is that business activity which concerns with the acquisition and conversation of capital funds in meeting financial needs and overall objectives of a business enterprise".

According to the **Guthumann and Dougall**, "Business finance can broadly be defined as the activity concerned with planning, raising, controlling, administering of the funds used in the business".

In the words of **Parhter and Wert**, "Business finance deals primarily with raising, administering and disbursing funds by privately owned business units operating in non-financial fields of industry".

Corporate finance is concerned with budgeting, financial forecasting, cash management, credit administration, investment analysis and fund procurement of the business concern and the business concern needs to adopt modern technology and application suitable to the global environment.

According to the **Encyclopedia of Social Sciences,**

"Corporation finance deals with the financial problems of corporate enterprises. These problems include the financial aspects of the promotion of new enterprises and their administration during early development, the accounting problems connected with the distinction between capital and income, the administrative questions created by growth and expansion, and finally, the financial adjustments required for the bolstering up or rehabilitation of a corporation which has come into financial difficulties".

TYPES OF FINANCE

Finance is one of the important and integral part of business concerns, hence, it plays a major role in every part of the business activities. It is used in all the area of the activities under the different names.

Finance can be classified into two major parts:

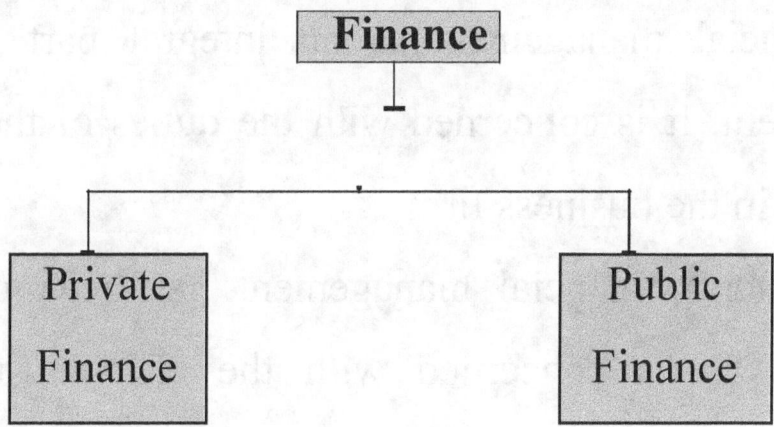

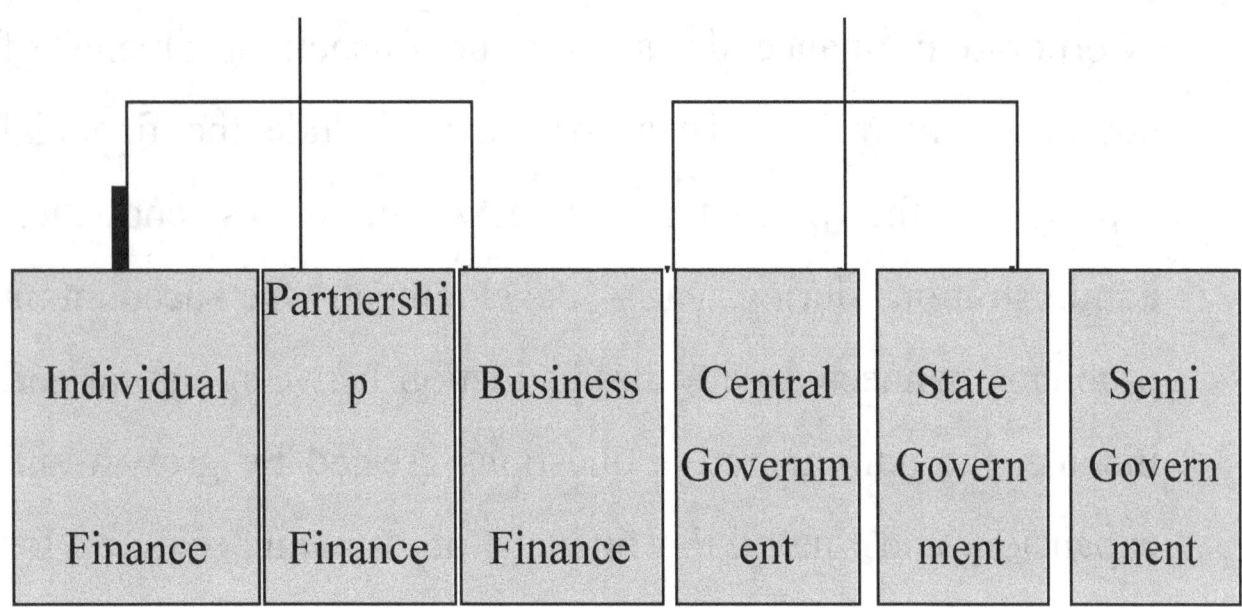

| Individual Finance | Partnership Finance | Business Finance | Central Government | State Government | Semi Government |

Fig. 1.1 *Types of Finance*

Private Finance, which includes the Individual, Firms, Business or Corporate Financial activities to meet the requirements. Public Finance which concerns with revenue and disbursement of Government such as Central Government, State Government and Semi-Government Financial matters.

DEFINITION OF FINANCIAL MANAGEMENT

Financial management is an integral part of overall management. It is concerned with the duties of the financial managers in the business firm.

The term financial management has been defined by **Solomon**, "It is concerned with the efficient use of an important economic resource namely, capital funds".

The most popular and acceptable definition of financial management as given by **S.C. Kuchal** is that "Financial Management deals with procurement of funds and their effective utilization in the business".

Howard and Upton : Financial management "as an application of general managerial principles to the area of financial decision-making.

Weston and Brigham : Financial management "is an area of financial decision-making, harmonizing individual motives and enterprise goals".

Joshep and Massie : Financial management "is the operational activity of a business that is responsible for obtaining and effectively utilizing the funds necessary for efficient operations.

Thus, Financial Management is mainly concerned with the effective funds management in the business. In simple words, Financial Management as practiced by business firms can be called as Corporation Finance or Business Finance.

SCOPE OF FINANCIAL MANAGEMENT

Financial management is one of the important parts of

overall management, which is directly related with various functional departments like personnel, marketing and production. Financial management covers wide area with multidimensional approaches. The following are the important scope of financial management.

1. Financial Management and Economics

Economic concepts like micro and macroeconomics are directly applied with the financial management approaches. Investment decisions, micro and macro environmental factors are closely associated with the functions of financial manager. Financial management also uses the economic equations like money value discount factor, economic order quantity etc. Financial economics is one of the emerging area, which provides immense opportunities to finance, and economical areas.

2. Financial Management and Accounting

Accounting records includes the financial information of the business concern. Hence, we can easily understand the relationship between the financial management and accounting. In the olden periods, both financial management and accounting are treated as a same discipline and then it has been merged as Management Accounting because this part is very much helpful to finance manager to take decisions. But nowaday's financial management and accounting discipline are separate and interrelated.

3. Financial Management or Mathematics

Modern approaches of the financial management applied large number of mathematical and statistical tools and techniques. They are also called as econometrics. Economic order quantity, discount factor, time value of money, present value of money, cost of capital, capital structure theories, dividend theories, ratio analysis and working capital analysis are used as mathematical and statistical tools and techniques in the field of financial management.

4. Financial Management and Production Management

Production management is the operational part of the business concern, which helps to multiple the money into profit. Profit of the concern depends upon the production performance. Production performance needs finance, because production department requires raw material, machinery, wages, operating expenses etc. These expenditures are decided and estimated by the financial department and the finance manager allocates the appropriate finance to production department. The financial manager must be aware of the operational process and finance required for each process of production activities.

5. Financial Management and Marketing

Produced goods are sold in the market with innovative and modern approaches. For this, the marketing department needs finance to meet their requirements.

The financial manager or finance department is responsible to allocate the adequate finance to the marketing department. Hence, marketing and financial management are interrelated and depends on each other.

6. Financial Management and Human Resource

Financial management is also related with human resource department, which provides manpower to all the functional areas of the management. Financial manager should carefully evaluate the requirement of manpower to each department and allocate the finance to the human resource department as wages, salary, remuneration, commission, bonus, pension and other monetary benefits to the human resource department. Hence, financial management is directly related with human resource management.

OBJECTIVES OF FINANCIAL MANAGEMENT

Effective procurement and efficient use of finance lead to proper utilization of the finance by the business concern. It is the essential part of the financial manager. Hence, the financial manager must determine the basic objectives of the financial management. Objectives of Financial Management may be broadly divided into two parts such as:

1. Profit maximization
2. Wealth maximization.

Profit Maximization

Main aim of any kind of economic activity is earning profit. A business concern is also functioning mainly for the purpose of earning profit. Profit is the measuring techniques to understand the business efficiency of the concern. Profit maximization is also the traditional and narrow approach, which aims at, maximizes the profit of the concern. Profit maximization consists of the following important features.

1. Profit maximization is also called as cashing per

share maximization. It leads to maximize the business operation for profit maximization.

2.   Ultimate aim of the business concern is earning profit, hence, it considers all the possible ways to increase the profitability of the concern.

3.   Profit is the parameter of measuring the efficiency of the business concern. So it shows the entire position of the business concern.

4.   Profit maximization objectives help to reduce the risk of the business.

Favourable Arguments for Profit Maximization

The following important points are in support of the profit maximization objectives of the business concern:

(i)   Main aim is earning profit.

(ii)   Profit is the parameter of the business operation.

(iii) Profit reduces risk of the business concern.

(iv)   Profit is the main source of finance.

(v)   Profitability meets the social needs also.

Unfavourable Arguments for Profit Maximization

The following important points are against the objectives

of profit maximization:

(i) Profit maximization leads to exploiting workers and consumers.

(ii) Profit maximization creates immoral practices such as corrupt practice, unfair trade practice, etc.

(iii) Profit maximization objectives leads to inequalities among the sake holders such as customers, suppliers, public shareholders, etc.

Drawbacks of Profit Maximization

Profit maximization objective consists of certain drawback also:

(i) **It is vague:** In this objective, profit is not defined precisely or correctly. It creates some unnecessary opinion regarding earning habits of the business concern.

(ii) **It ignores the time value of money:** Profit maximization does not consider the time value of money or the net present value of the cash inflow. It leads certain differences between the actual cash inflow and net present cash flow during a particular period.

(iii) **It ignores risk:** Profit maximization does not consider risk of the business concern. Risks may be internal or external which will affect the overall operation of the business concern.

Wealth Maximization

Wealth maximization is one of the modern approaches, which involves latest innovations and improvements in the field of the business concern. The term wealth means shareholder wealth or the wealth of the persons those who are involved in the business concern.

Wealth maximization is also known as value maximization or net present worth maximization. This objective is an universally accepted concept in the field of business.

Favourable Arguments for Wealth Maximization

(i) Wealth maximization is superior to the profit maximization because the main aim of the business concern under this concept is to improve the value or wealth of the shareholders.

(ii) Wealth maximization considers the comparison of the value to cost associated with the business concern. Total value detected from the total cost incurred for the business operation. It provides extract value of the business concern.

(iii) Wealth maximization considers both time and risk of the business concern.

(iv) Wealth maximization provides efficient allocation of resources.

(v) It ensures the economic interest of the society.

Unfavourable Arguments for Wealth Maximization

(i) Wealth maximization leads to prescriptive idea of the business concern but it may not be suitable to present day business activities.

(ii) Wealth maximization is nothing, it is also profit maximization, it is the indirect name of the profit maximization.

(iii) Wealth maximization creates ownership-management controversy.

(iv) Management alone enjoy certain benefits.

(v) The ultimate aim of the wealth maximization objectives is to maximize the profit.

(vi) Wealth maximization can be activated only with the help of the profitable position of the business concern.

APPROACHES TO FINANCIAL MANAGEMENT

Financial management approach measures the scope of the financial management in various fields, which include the essential part of the finance. Financial management is not a revolutionary concept but an evolutionary. The definition and scope of financial management has been changed from one period to another period and applied various innovations. Theoretical points of view, financial management approach may be broadly divided into two major parts.

Traditional Approach

Traditional approach is the initial stage of financial management, which was followed, in the early part of during the year 1920 to 1950. This approach is based on the past experience and the traditionally accepted methods. Main part of the traditional approach is rising of funds for the business concern. Traditional approach consists of the following important area.

Arrangement of funds from lending body.

Arrangement of funds through various financial instruments.

Finding out the various sources of funds.

FUNCTIONS OF FINANCE MANAGER

Finance function is one of the major parts of business organization, which involves the permanent, and continuous process of the business concern. Finance is one of the interrelated functions which deal with personal function, marketing function, production function and research and development activities of the business concern. At present, every business concern concentrates more on the field of finance because, it is a very emerging part which reflects the entire operational and profit ability position of the concern. Deciding the proper financial function is the essential and ultimate goal of the business organization.

Finance manager is one of the important role players in the field of finance function. He must have entire knowledge in the area of accounting, finance, economics and management. His position is highly critical and analytical to solve various problems related to finance. A person who deals finance related activities may be called finance manager.

Finance manager performs the following major functions:

1.   Forecasting Financial Requirements

It is the primary function of the Finance Manager. He is responsible to estimate the financial requirement of the business concern. He should estimate, how much finances required to acquire fixed assets and forecast the amount needed to meet the working capital requirements in future.

2. Acquiring Necessary Capital

After deciding the financial requirement, the finance manager should concentrate how the finance is mobilized and where it will be available. It is also highly critical in nature.

3. Investment Decision

The finance manager must carefully select best investment alternatives and consider the reasonable and stable return from the investment. He must be well versed in the field of capital budgeting techniques to determine the effective utilization of investment. The finance manager must concentrate to principles of safety, liquidity and profitability while investing capital.

4. Cash Management

Present days cash management plays a major role in the

area of finance because proper cash management is not only essential for effective utilization of cash but it also helps to meet the short-term liquidity position of the concern.

5. Interrelation with Other Departments

Finance manager deals with various functional departments such as marketing, production, personel, system, research, development, etc. Finance manager should have sound knowledge not only in finance related area but also well versed in other areas. He must maintain a good relationship with all the functional departments of the business organization.

IMPORTANCE OF FINANCIAL MANAGEMENT

Finance is the lifeblood of business organization. It needs to meet the requirement of the business concern. Each and every business concern must maintain adequate amount of finance for their smooth running of the business concern and also maintain the business carefully to achieve the goal of the business concern. The business goal can be achieved only with the help of effective management of finance. We can't neglect the importance of finance at any time at and at any situation. Some of the importance of the financial management is as follows:

Financial Planning

Financial management helps to determine the financial requirement of the business concern and leads to take financial planning of the concern. Financial planning is an important part of the business concern, which helps to promotion of an enterprise.

Acquisition of Funds

Financial management involves the acquisition of required finance to the business concern. Acquiring needed funds play a major part of the financial management, which involve possible source of finance at minimum cost.

Proper Use of Funds

Proper use and allocation of funds leads to improve the operational efficiency of the business concern. When the finance manager uses the funds properly, they can reduce the cost of capital and increase the value of the firm.

Financial Decision

Financial management helps to take sound financial decision in the business concern. Financial decision will affect the entire business operation of the concern. Because there is a direct relationship with various department functions such as marketing, production personnel, etc.

Improve Profitability

Profitability of the concern purely depends on the effectiveness and proper utilization of funds by the business concern. Financial management helps to improve the profitability position of the concern with the help of strong financial control devices such as budgetary control, ratio analysis and cost volume profit analysis.

Increase the Value of the Firm

Financial management is very important in the field of increasing the wealth of the investors and the business concern. Ultimate aim of any business concern will achieve the maximum profit and higher profitability leads to maximize the wealth of the investors as well as the nation.

Promoting Savings

Savings are possible only when the business concern earns higher profitability and maximizing wealth. Effective financial management helps to promoting and mobilizing individual and corporate savings.

Nowadays financial management is also popularly known as business finance or corporate finances. The business concern or corporate sectors cannot function without the importance of the financial management.

MODEL QUESTIONS

1. What is finance? Define business finance.

2. Explain the types of finance.

3. Discuss the objectives of financial management.

4. Critically evaluate various approaches to the financial management.

5. Explain the scope of financial management.

6. Discuss the role of financial manager.

7. Explain the importance of financial management.

Chapter 02

Financial Statement Analysis

FINANACIAL ANALYSIS

Financial analysis is the art and science of examining and drawing inferences from the financial statements. Financial analysis is also known as analysis and interpretation of financial statements. It refers to the process of determining financial strengths and weaknesses of the firm by studying the relationship between the items of balance sheet, profit & loss account and the other operative data. Financial analysis is largely a study of relationship among the various financial factors in a business as disclosed by a single set of statements and a study of these factors as shown in a series of statements.

FINANCIAL STATEMENT

The term "Financial Statements" as used in modern business refers to two statements which the accountant prepares at the end of a period of time. They are balance sheet and Income statement. There are some other statements which are not only important but are essential for the business enterprise to draw useful conclusions regarding the financial position of the concern.

In the words of Hampton, "A financial statement is an organized collection of data organized according to logical and consistent accounting procedures."

In the word of Howard and Upton, "Although any formal financial statements expressed in money values might be thought of as financial statements, the term has come to be limited by most accounting and business writers to mean the „balance sheet" and the „profit and loss statements".

FINANCIAL STATEMENT ANALYSIS

Financial Statement Analysis is an analysis which highlights important relationships in the financial statements. Financial statement analysis embraces the methods used in assessing and interpreting the results of past performance and current financial position as they relate to particular factors of interest of past performance and current financial position as they relate to particular factors of interest in investment decisions. It is an important means of assessing past performance and in forecasting and planning future performance.

Financial Statement Analysis is an information processing system designed to provide data for decision-making model, bank lending decision models, and corporate financial management models.

TYPES OF FINANCIAL STATEMENTS

There are two major financial statements which are vital to financial analysis and financial management i.e., profit and loss account and balance sheet. These statements contain various information's often needed by various persons interested in the enterprise such as shareholder, government, debenture holder, management etc. They convey the financial condition and results of an enterprise for a given period and at a given date. In annual report, together with these two statements, there may be statement or schedules of retained earnings, stockholders, equity statement, capital surplus fund, cash flow statement etc. Accounting is a language of „Finance" or „Monetary". A general search continues to be made for ways to improve readability of financial statements.

A lay man who read these statements is not able to understand the terminology used in these statements.

➤ BALANCE SHEET

The balance sheet is a statement of assets and liabilities of a firm or what it owns and what it owes, as on a given date. In a balance sheet, the assets and liabilities are equal to each other. In the word of Pyle, White and Larson, "A balance sheet is so called because its two sides must always balance, the sum of the assets shown on the balance sheet must equal liabilities plus owner equity. According to Block and Hirt, "The balance sheet indicates what the firm owns and how these assets are financed in the form of liabilities or ownership interest".

It is a statement of affairs of an organization at a point of time and may be defined as a statement prepared with a view to measuring the financial position of a business enterprise at a certain fixed date. In reveals the financial position of a business as reflected by the accounting records and contains a list of assets, liability and capital items as on a given date. The balance sheet is designed to show the condition of the business in a form easily readable and more quickly comprehended that would be possible form a survey of the facts shown in the detailed records. The intention is to afford the shareholders who have placed their capital in an enterprise and the creditor who does business with it, an opportunity of estimating from time to time the financial stability.

The balance sheet is also known as „Statement of Financial Condition", „Statement of Financial Position", „Statement of Assets and Liabilities", „Statements of Resources and Liabilities", Statement of Assets, Liabilities and Capital", „Statement of Worth", and „Financial Statement". It is a Hastings, "It reveals the property owned by the business, the assets and the debts owned by the company, the liabilities."

➤ INCOME STATEMENT

The income statement, usually designated as profit and loss account for the relevant financial year, shows the net profit or net loss resulting from the operations of business during a special field period of time. The items appearing in it are in the nature of „revenue". In the words of Walgenbech, Dittrich and Hanson, "To show the results of operations for a period, an income statement is prepared, which lists the revenues and expenses and resents the resulting net income amount.

Foulke defines income statement as "the mathematical interpretation of the policies, experience, knowledge, foresight, and aggressiveness of the management of a business enterprise from the point of view of income, expenses, gross margin, operating profit, and net profit or loss."

Provides a review of the factors directly concerned with the determination of the net income- the revenue realized from the sale of goods or services and the costs incurred in the process of producing the revenue. The income statement summarizes the changes that have taken place since the date of preceding balance sheet and that have affected the owner's share in the business either by gain or loss. It is a performance report recording the changes in income, expenses, profit and loss as a result of business operations during the year between two balance sheet dates.

USERS OF FINANCIAL STATEMENTS

☞ Management

☞ Investors

☞ Bankers

☞ Government

☞ Research scholar

☞ Trade creditors

☞ Labour unions

☞ Public

☞ **<u>MANAGEMENT</u>**

Financial statements are of very great help to management in understanding the progress, position and prospects of business. Using analogy, it can be said that financial statements serve the business management as gauges and charts serve the engineer. In the absence of information's which are included in the financial statements, management can neither plan nor fulfill easily the functions of operation and control.

☞ **<u>INVESTORS</u>**

Financial statements are also significant for investor both present and prospective. However, the investors look to the financial position of business concern from a different angle. Investors are interested in two things-firstly; they want to invest in such a situation where they feel the financial structure of a company is sound. Secondly, they want to invest only in such concern whose future is bright. Investor gives first attention to the profits after taxes in the profit and loss account. In case of prospective potential investment opportunity.

☞ **BANKERS**

A banker is primarily concerned with the ability of paying current debts and the current operation results. He wants not only the payment of advances but he also wants that such advance should be repaid at proper time also.

☞ **GOVERNMENT**

Central and State Governments and Local Authorities are also interested in published financial statements in order to assess their revenues through various taxes to regulate capital issue and public utility regulation.

☞ **RESEARCH SCHOLARS**

The financial analysis and research workers are interested in published financial statements for guiding management or for establishing certain principles. A financial analyst can peep through these statements into the financial policies pursued by the management and offer constructive suggestions to overcome the financial malady, if diagnosed.

☞ TRADE CREDITORS

From the creditors point of view the financial statements act as magic eye highlighting the credit worthiness, i.e., assurance whether the company will honor obligations as and when they mature.

☞ LABOUR UNIONS

From social justice point of view in the present time, the labour unions may know now if the labour is getting its fair share of business earnings.

☞ PUBLIC

Financial Statements are also valuable to the public who are interested in prospects of a concern, in one way or the other. It is the securities of the enterprise alone that are bought and sold on stock exchanges and the public is interested, mostly in their financial standing and also to avoid hostile feelings of the public.

TECHNIQUES OF FINANCIAL STATEMENT ANALYSIS

The Analysis consists of the study of inter-relationship between various items comprised in financial statements to determine whether the earnings and the financial position of the company are satisfactory. A number of techniques are used in the analysis of financial statements, some of which are as follows:

➥ Comparative Financial Statements

➥ Common-size Statements

➥ Trend Analysis

➥ Fund-flow Analysis

➥ Cash-flow Analysis

➥ Value-added Statement

➥ Ratio Analysis

COMPARATIVE FINANCIAL STATEMENTS

Comparison of financial statements for two or more years is another technique used in analyzing data. Comparative financial statements are statements of financial position of a business so designed as to provide time perspective to the consideration of various elements of financial position embodied in such statements. For this purpose the balance sheet and profit and loss account are prepared in comparative form. Comparative Statements may be made to show:

(i) Absolute date (rupee amount or money values),

(ii) Increase or decrease in absolute values data in terms of money values and

(iii) Increase or decrease in absolute data in terms of percentage.

COMMON-SIZE STATEMENTS

In order to avoid the limitations of Comparative Statement, this type of analysis is designed. Under this method, financial statements are analyzed to measure the relationship of various figures with some common base. Accordingly, while preparing the Common Size Profit and Loss Account, total sales are taken as common base and other items are expressed as a percentage of sales. Like this, in order to prepare the Common Size Balance Sheet, the total assets or total liabilities are taken as common base and all other items are expressed as a percentage of total assets and liabilities.

TREND ANALYSIS

Trend Analysis is one of the important technique which is used for analysis and interpretations of financial statements. While applying this method, it is necessary to select a period for a number of years in order to ascertain the percentage relationship of various items in the financial statements comparing with the items in base year. When a trend is to be determined by applying this method, earliest year or first year is taken as the base year. The related items in the base year are taken as 100 and based on this trend percentage of corresponding figures of financial statements in the other years are concluded. This analysis is useful in framing suitable policies and forecasting in future also.

FUND FLOW ANALYSIS

Fund Flow Analysis is one of the important methods for analysis and interpretations of financial statements. This is the statement which acts as a supplementary statement to the profit and loss account and balance sheet. Fund Flow Analysis helps to determine the changes in financial position on working capital basis and on cash basis. It also reveals the information about the sources of funds and has been utilized or employed during particular period.

CASH FLOW ANALYSIS

The fund flow statement indicated changes in working capital which have taken place during the year. But the management is more interested in the changes in the cash inflow and outflow in the short run. It is historical statement which indicates the cash inflows and outflows during the last year and would guide management in framing policy regarding cash management. The cash budget shows the projected inflow and outflow of cash for the future budget period, while the cash flow statement is prepared on basis of historical financial statements.

VALUE ADDED STATEMENT

The value added technique to judge the efficiency of an enterprise is at its intact in India. It indicates the net value or wealth created by the manufacturer during a specific period. No enterprise can survive or grow, if it fails to generate wealth. An enterprise may exist without making profit but cannot survive without adding value. The enterprise, not making profit, shall become sick but not adding value may cause its death over a period of time. Thus the value added is basic and broad measure of judging the performance of an enterprise.

RATIO ANALYSIS

To evaluate the financial condition and performance of an enterprise, the financial analyst needs certain yardsticks frequently used is a ratio, or index, relating two pieces of financial data to each other. Ratios, as a tool of financial management, can be expressed as (a) percentage, (b) fraction, and (c) a stated comparison between numbers. According to Batty, "The term „accounting ratios" is used describe significant relationship which exist between figures shown on a balance sheet, in as profit and loss account, in a budgetary control system, or in any other part of the accounting organization."

Financial ratios can be divided into certain categories on the basis of the items which are used for ratios. Four types of financial ratios are commonly used:

(1) Profitability ratios,

(2) Liquidity ratios,

(3) Solvency ratios, and

(4) Activity ratios.

Chapter 03
Ratio Analysis

Introduction

Ratio analysis is a commonly used tool of financial statement analysis. Ratio is a mathematical relationship between one number to another number. Ratio is used as an index for evaluating the financial performance of the business concern. An accounting ratio shows the mathematical relationship between two figures, which have meaningful relation with each other. Ratio can be classified into various types. Classification from the point of view of financial management is as follows:

(1) Profitability ratios,

(2) Liquidity ratios,

(3) Solvency ratios, and

(4) Activity ratios.

PROFITABILITY RATIOS

Every business unit is established to earn profit and develop on that basis. Hence, the profitability ratios are the most important ratios. The management of business should find out profitability ratios to evaluate their own performance and to get an idea of progress of their business. The shareholders who have invested their money in the company's business, desire to get good return on their investment. Creditors are also interested in profitability, as it will assure them of interest being paid to them in time and also of principal amount being returned to them on time. This is possible only when business is profitable.

✓ **Gross Profit Ratio**

It is a ratio expressing relationship between Gross Profit earned to Net Sales. It is a useful indication of the profitability of business. This ratio is usually expressed as a percentage. This ratio shows whether mark-up obtained on cost of production is sufficient. There is no standard showing reasonableness of gross profit ratio. However, it must be enough to cover its operating expenses. If this ratio is low, it indicates that the cost of sales is high or that the purchasing is inefficient. Alternatively, it may also mean that due to depression, the selling price is reduced but there may be no corresponding reduction in cost of sales. In such a case, the management must investigate the causes and try to bring up this ratio.

Gross Profit Ratio = Gross Profit / Sales * 100

✓ Net Profit Ratio

The ratio is valuable for the purpose of ascertaining the over-all profitability of business and shows the efficiency or otherwise of operating the business. Generally, the ratio is computed on the basis of net profit earned from operation of business and non-operating expenses and incomes are excluded. Generally, tax is deducted from profit while calculating this ratio. This ratio indicates what portion of sales revenue is left to the proprietors after all operating expenses are met. The higher this ratio, the better will be the profitability.

Net Profit Ratio = Net Profit / Net Sales *100

✓ Return on Shareholders' Fund

In order to judge the efficiency with which the proprietors" funds are employed in business, this ratio is ascertained. Proprietors" Equity or Proprietors" Funds include share capital and reserves. It indicates whether the return on proprietors" funds is enough relation to the risks that they undertake. This ratio shows what amount of dividend is likely to be received on shares. Naturally when return on shareholders' funds is to be calculated, the profit should be after interest and tax. This ratio is usually expressed in percentage.

Return on Shareholders'Funds = Net Profit / ShareholdersFunds*100

✓ **Earnings per Share (EPS)**

This ratio measures the profit available to equity shareholders on per share basis. It is not the actual amount paid to shareholders as dividend but it is the maximum that can be paid to them. It is calculated by the number of equity shares. Here the profit available to equity shareholder is after-tax profit deducting the preference dividend. The ratio shows the profitability of the firm from the owners" point of view. By comparing the EPS of the current year with those of past few years the trend of profitability can be ascertained.

Earnings per share (EPS) = Profit after tax – Pref. Dividend / No. of Equity Shares

❖ LIQUIDITY RATIO

These ratios indicate the position of liquidity. They are computed to ascertain whether the company is capable of meeting of short term obligations from its short term resources. Cash on hand, bank balance, bills receivable, debtors etc. are such assets which are readily available for paying current liabilities as and when they arise. Where such assets are in sufficient proportion as compared to current liabilities, the "Liquid position" of business is said to be satisfactory.

✓ Current Ratio

This most widely used ratio shows the proportion of current assets to current liabilities. It is also known as "Working Capital Ratio" as it is a measure of working capital available at a particular time. The ratio is obtained by dividing current assets by the current liabilities. It is measure of short-term financial strength of the business and shows whether the business will be able to meet its current liabilities, as and when they mature. Liability which will mature within a period of 12 months is a current liability. They include creditors, bills payable, bank overdraft, outstanding expenses, provision for taxation etc. Similarly, current assets are in the form of cash or can be readily converted into cash within a short time. They include cash, bank balance, bills receivable, prepaid expenses, accrued income, readily marketable securities etc.

Current Ratio = Current Assets / Current Liabilities

✓ Quick Ratio

The measure of absolute liquidity may be obtained by comparing by only cash and bank balance as well as readily marketable securities with liquid liabilities. This is a very exacting standard of liquidity and it is satisfactory it the ratio is 0.5: 1. It is computed by dividing the value of quick assets by liquid liabilities. Here, quick assets do not include both stock and debtors, because payments from debtors would not generally be received immediately when liquid liabilities are to be paid. Thus the quick assets comprise only cash balance, bank balance and readily marketable securities only.

Quick Ratio = Quick Assets / Liquid Liabilities

❖ SOLVENCY RATIO

The term 'Solvency' generally refers to the capacity of the business to meet its short-term and long-term obligations.

Short-term obligations include creditors, bank loans and bills payable etc. Long-term obligations consist of debenture, long-term loans and long-term creditors etc. Solvency Ratio indicates the sound financial position of a concern to carry on its business smoothly and meet its all obligations.

✓ Debt-Equity Ratio

This ratio indicates the degree of financial leverage being used by the business and includes both short-term and long-term debt. A rising debt-to-equity ratio implies higher interest expenses, and beyond a certain point it may affect a company's credit rating, making it more expensive to raise more debt. A higher ratio means that outside creditors have a larger claim than the owners of the business. The pressure from creditors would increase and their interference will also increase. The company with high-debt position will have to accept stricter conditions from the lenders, while borrowing money. If this ratio is lower, it is not profitable form the viewpoint of equity shareholders, as benefit of trading on equity is not availed of and the rate of equity dividend will be comparatively lower.

Debt to equity = Total debt / Total equity

✓ Debt to Assets Ratio

Debt to Assets Ratio is to compare Total Assets with Total Debts. This is called Total Debt to Assets Ratio. Here, both long-term and short-term debts are aggregated and divided by total assets employed in business. It indicates the proportion of debts, in the total assets used in business. The lower ratio is beneficial from viewpoint of creditors while higher ratio increases the risk of creditors.

Debt to Assets Ratio = Total Debt / Total Assets

❖ EFFICIENCY RATIO

The ratios which show the efficiency with which assets are used in business are known as Activity Ratios or Turnover Ratios or Efficiency ratios. Such ratios show the speed with which assets are converted into ash as compared to sales. The higher these ratios, the higher are the efficiency of business. Creditors and shareholder invest their money for investing in assets of business and so they are interested in knowing the efficiency and speed with which the assets are converted into sales. Some proportion must be maintained between sales and total assets.

✓ <u>**Stock Turnover Ratio**</u>

The number of times the average stock is turned over during the year is known as stock turnover. It is computed by dividing the cost of goods sold by the average stock in the business. Average stock is the average of opening and closing stock of the year. This ratio is very important in judging the ability of management with which it can move the stock. The higher the turnover ratio, the more profitable the business would be.

Stock Turnover Ratio = Cost of Goods Sold / Average Stock

✓ <u>**Fixed Assets Turnover**</u>

To ascertain the efficiency and profitability of business, the total fixed assets are compared to sales. The more the sales in relation to the amount invested in fixed assets, the more efficient is the use of fixed assets. It indicates higher efficiency. If the sales are less as compared to investment in fixed assets, it means that fixed assets are not adequately utilized in business. Excessive sale is an indication of aver trading and is dangerous.

Fixed Assets Turnover = Sales / Fixed Assets

MODEL QUESTIONS

1. What is financial statement?

2. What is financial statement analysis?

3. Discuss various types of financial statement analysis.

4. Explain various methods of financial statement analysis.

5. What are the differences between fund flow and cash flow?

6. What is Ratio Analysis ? Explain its types?

Chapter 04
Sources of Financing

INTRODUCTION

Finance is the lifeblood of business concern, because it is interlinked with all activities performed by the business concern. In a human body, if blood circulation is not proper, body function will stop. Similarly, if the finance not being properly arranged, the business system will stop. Arrangement of the required finance to each department of business concern is highly a complex one and it needs careful decision. Quantum of finance may be depending upon the nature and situation of the business concern. But, the requirement of the finance may be broadly classified into two parts:

Long-term Financial Requirements or Fixed Capital Requirement

Financial requirement of the business differs from firm to firm and the nature of the requirements on the basis of terms or period of financial requirement, it may be long term and short-term financial requirements.

Long-term financial requirement means the finance needed to acquire land and building for business concern, purchase of plant and machinery and other fixed expenditure. Long-term financial requirement is also called as fixed capital requirements. Fixed capital is the capital, which is used to purchase the fixed assets of the firms such as land and building, furniture and fittings, plant and machinery, etc. Hence, it is also called a capital expenditure.

Short-term Financial Requirements or Working Capital Requirement

Apart from the capital expenditure of the firms, the firms should need certain expenditure like procurement of raw materials, payment of wages, day-to-day expenditures, etc. This kind of expenditure is to meet with the help of short-term financial requirements which will meet the operational expenditure of the firms. Short-term financial requirements are popularly known as working capital.

SOURCES OF FINANCE

Sources of finance mean the ways for mobilizing various terms of finance to the industrial concern. Sources of finance state that, how the companies are mobilizing finance for their requirements. The companies belong to the existing or the new which need sum amount of finance to meet the long-term and short-term requirements such as purchasing of fixed assets, construction of office building, purchase of raw materials and day-to-day expenses.

Sources of finance may be classified under various categories according to the following important heads:

1. Based on the Period

Sources of Finance may be classified under various categories based on the period.

Long-term sources: Finance may be mobilized by long-term or short-term. When the finance mobilized with large amount and the repayable over the period will be more than five years, it may be considered as long-term sources. Share capital, issue of debenture, long-term loans from financial institutions and commercial banks come under this kind of source of finance. Long-term source of finance needs to meet the capital expenditure of the firms such as purchase of fixed assets, land and buildings, etc.

Long-term sources of finance include:

- Equity Shares
- Preference Shares
- Debenture
- Long-term Loans
- Fixed Deposits

Short-term sources: Apart from the long-term source of finance, firms can generate finance with the help of short-term sources like loans and advances from commercial banks, moneylenders, etc. Short-term source of finance needs to meet the operational expenditure of the business concern.

Short-term source of finance include:

- Bank Credit
- Customer Advances
- Trade Credit
- Factoring
- Public Deposits
- Money Market Instruments

2. Based on Ownership

Sources of Finance may be classified under various categories based on the period:

An ownership source of finance include

- Shares capital, earnings
- Retained earnings
- Surplus and Profits

Borrowed capital include

- Debenture
- Bonds
- Public deposits
- Loans from Bank and Financial Institutions.

3.   Based on Sources of Generation

Sources of Finance may be classified into various categories based on the period.

Internal source of finance includes

- Retained earnings
- Depreciation funds
- Surplus

External sources of finance may be include

- Share capital
- Debenture
- Public deposits
- Loans from Banks and Financial institutions

4.   Based in Mode of Finance Security finance may be

include

- Shares capital
- Debenture

Retained earnings may include

- Retained earnings
- Depreciation funds

Loan finance may include

- Long-term loans from Financial Institutions
- Short-term loans from Commercial banks.

The above classifications are based on the nature and how the finance is mobilized from various sources. But the above sources of finance can be divided into three major classifications:

- Security Finance
- Internal Finance
- Loans Finance

SECURITY FINANCE

If the finance is mobilized through issue of securities such as shares and debenture, it is called as security finance. It is also called as corporate securities. This type of finance plays a major role in the field of deciding the capital structure of the company.

Characters of Security Finance

Security finance consists of the following important characters:

1. Long-term sources of finance.

2. It is also called as corporate securities.

3. Security finance includes both shares and debentures.

4. It plays a major role in deciding the capital structure of the company.

5. Repayment of finance is very limited.

6. It is a major part of the company's total capitalization.

Types of Security Finance

Security finance may be divided into two major types:

1. Ownership securities or capital stock.

2. Creditorship securities or debt capital.

Ownership Securities

The ownership securities also called as capital stock, is commonly called as shares. Shares are the most Universal method of raising finance for the business concern. Ownership capital consists of the following types of securities.

- Equity Shares

- Preference Shares
- No par stock
- Deferred Shares

EQUITY SHARES

Equity Shares also known as ordinary shares, which means, other than preference shares. Equity shareholders are the real owners of the company. They have a control over the management of the company. Equity shareholders are eligible to get dividend if the company earns profit. Equity share capital cannot be redeemed during the lifetime of the company. The liability of the equity shareholders is the value of unpaid value of shares.

Features of Equity Shares

Equity shares consist of the following important features:

1. **Maturity of the shares:** Equity shares have permanent nature of capital, which has no maturity period. It cannot be redeemed during the lifetime of the company.

2. **Residual claim on income:** Equity shareholders have the right to get income left after paying fixed rate of dividend to preference shareholder. The earnings or the income available to the shareholders is equal to the profit after tax minus preference dividend.

3. **Residual claims on assets:** If the company wound up, the ordinary or equity shareholders have the right to get the claims on assets. These rights are only available to the equity shareholders.

4. **Right to control:** Equity shareholders are the real owners of the company. Hence, they have power to control the management of the company and they have power to take any decision regarding the business operation.

5. **Voting rights:** Equity shareholders have voting rights in the meeting of the company with the help of voting right power; they can change or remove any decision of the business concern. Equity shareholders only have voting rights in the company meeting and also they can nominate proxy to participate and vote in the meeting instead of the shareholder.

6. **Pre-emptive right:** Equity shareholder pre-emptive rights. The pre-emptive right is the legal right of the existing shareholders. It is attested by the company in the first opportunity to purchase additional equity shares in proportion to their current holding capacity.

7. **Limited liability:** Equity shareholders are having only limited liability to the value of shares they have purchased. If the shareholders are having fully paid up shares, they have no liability. For example: If the shareholder purchased 100 shares with the face value of Rs. 10 each. He paid only Rs. 900. His liability is only Rs. 100.

Advantages of Equity Shares

Equity shares are the most common and universally used shares to mobilize finance for the company. It consists of the following advantages.

1.   **Permanent sources of finance:** Equity share capital is belonging to long-term permanent nature of sources of finance, hence, it can be used for long-term or fixed capital requirement of the business concern.

2.   **Voting rights:** Equity shareholders are the real owners of the company who have voting rights. This type of advantage is available only to the equity shareholders.

No fixed dividend: Equity shares do not create any obligation to pay a fixed rate of dividend. If the company earns profit, equity shareholders are eligible for profit, they are eligible to get dividend otherwise, and they cannot claim any dividend from the company.

4.   **Less cost of capital:** Cost of capital is the major factor, which affects the value of the company. If the company wants

to increase the value of the company, they have to use more share capital because, it consists of less cost of capital (K_e) while compared to other sources of finance.

5. **Retained earnings:** When the company have more share capital, it will be suitable for retained earnings which is the less cost sources of finance while compared to other sources of finance.

Disadvantages of Equity Shares

1. **Irredeemable:** Equity shares cannot be redeemed during the lifetime of the business concern. It is the most dangerous thing of over capitalization.

2. **Obstacles in management:** Equity shareholder can put obstacles in management by manipulation and organizing themselves. Because, they have power to contrast any decision which are against the wealth of the shareholders.

3. **Leads to speculation:** Equity shares dealings in share market lead to secularism during prosperous periods.

4. **Limited income to investor:** The Investors who desire to invest in safe securities with a fixed income have no attraction for equity shares.

5. **No trading on equity:** When the company raises capital

only with the help of equity, the company cannot take the advantage of trading on equity.

PREFERENCE SHARES

The parts of corporate securities are called as preference shares. It is the shares, which have preferential right to get dividend and get back the initial investment at the time of winding up of the company. Preference shareholders are eligible to get fixed rate of dividend and they do not have voting rights. Preference shares may be classified into the following major types:

1.   Cumulative preference shares: Cumulative preference shares have right to claim dividends for those years which have no profits. If the company is unable to earn profit in any one or more years, C.P. Shares are unable to get any dividend but they have right to get the comparative dividend for the previous years if the company earned profit.

2. Non-cumulative preference shares: Non-cumulative preference shares have no right to enjoy the above benefits. They are eligible to get only dividend if the company earns profit during the years. Otherwise, they cannot claim any dividend.

3.Redeemable preference shares: When, the preference shares have a fixed maturity period it becomes redeemable preference shares. It can be redeemable during the lifetime of the company. The Company Act has provided certain restrictions on the return of the redeemable preference shares.

Irredeemable Preference Shares

Irredeemable preference shares can be redeemed only when the company goes for liquidator. There is no fixed maturity period for such kind of preference shares.

Participating Preference Shares

Participating preference sharesholders have right to participate extra profits after distributing the equity shareholders.

Non-Participating Preference Shares

Non-participating preference sharesholders are not having any right to participate extra profits after distributing to the equity shareholders. Fixed rate of dividend is payable to the type of shareholders.

Convertible Preference Shares

Convertible preference sharesholders have right to convert their holding into equity shares after a specific period. The articles of association must authorize the right of conversion.

Non-convertible Preference Shares

There shares, cannot be converted into equity shares from preference shares.

Features of Preference Shares

The following are the important features of the preference shares:

1. **Maturity period:** Normally preference shares have no fixed maturity period except in the case of redeemable preference shares. Preference shares can be redeemable only at the time of the company liquidation.

2. **Residual claims on income:** Preferential sharesholders have a residual claim on income. Fixed rate of dividend is payable to the preference shareholders.

3. **Residual claims on assets:** The first preference is given to the preference shareholders at the time of liquidation. If any extra Assets are available that should be distributed to equity shareholder.

4. **Control of Management:** Preference shareholder does not have any voting rights. Hence, they cannot have control over the management of the company.

Advantages of Preference Shares

Preference shares have the following important advantages.

1.   **Fixed dividend:** The dividend rate is fixed in the case of preference shares. It is called as fixed income security because it provides a constant rate of income to the investors.

2.   **Cumulative dividends:** Preference shares have another advantage which is called cumulative dividends. If the company does not earn any profit in any previous years, it can be cumulative with future period dividend.

3.   **Redemption:** Preference Shares can be redeemable after a specific period except in the case of irredeemable preference shares. There is a fixed maturity period for repayment of the initial investment.

4.   **Participation:** Participative preference sharesholders can participate in the surplus profit after distribution to the equity shareholders.

5.   **Convertibility:** Convertibility preference shares can be converted into equity shares when the articles of association provide such conversion.

Disadvantages of Preference Shares

1.   **Expensive sources of finance:** Preference shares have high expensive source of finance while compared to equity shares.

2. **No voting right:** Generally preference sharesholders do not have any voting rights. Hence they cannot have the control over the management of the company.

3. **Fixed dividend only:** Preference shares can get only fixed rate of dividend. They may not enjoy more profits of the company.

4. **Permanent burden:** Cumulative preference shares become a permanent burden so far as the payment of dividend is concerned. Because the company must pay the dividend for the unprofitable periods also.

5. **Taxation:** In the taxation point of view, preference shares dividend is not a deductible expense while calculating tax. But, interest is a deductible expense. Hence, it has disadvantage on the tax deduction point of view.

DEFERRED SHARES

Deferred shares also called as founder shares because these shares were normally issued to founders. The shareholders have a preferential right to get dividend before the preference shares and equity shares. According to Companies Act 1956 no public limited company or which is a subsidiary of a public company can issue deferred shares.

These shares were issued to the founder at small

denomination to control over the management by the virtue of their voting rights.

NO PAR SHARES

When the shares are having no face value, it is said to be no par shares. The company issues this kind of shares which is divided into a number of specific shares without any specific denomination. The value of shares can be measured by dividing the real net worth of the company with the total number of shares.

CREDITORSHIP SECURITIES

Creditorship Securities also known as debt finance which means the finance is mobilized from the creditors. Debenture and Bonds are the two major parts of the Creditorship Securities.

Debentures

A Debenture is a document issued by the company. It is a certificate issued by the company under its seal acknowledging a debt.

According to the Companies Act 1956, "debenture includes debenture stock, bonds and any other securities of a company whether constituting a charge of the assets of the company or not."

[63]

Types of Debentures

Debentures may be divided into the following major types:

1. **Unsecured debentures:** Unsecured debentures are not given any security on assets of the company. It is also called simple or naked debentures. This type of debentures are treaded as unsecured creditors at the time of winding up of the company.

2. **Secured debentures:** Secured debentures are given security on assets of the company. It is also called as mortgaged debentures because these debentures are given against any mortgage of the assets of the company.

3. **Redeemable debentures:** These debentures are to be redeemed on the expiry of a certain period. The interest is paid periodically and the initial investment is returned after the fixed maturity period.

4. **Irredeemable debentures:** These kind of debentures cannot be redeemable during the life time of the business concern.

5. **Convertible debentures:** Convertible debentures are the debentures whose holders have the option to get them converted wholly or partly into shares. These debentures are usually converted into equity shares. Conversion of the

debentures may be:

Non-convertible debentures Fully convertible debentures Partly convertible debentures

6.   **Other types:** Debentures can also be classified into the following types. Some of the common types of the debentures are as follows:

1.   Collateral Debenture

2.   Guaranteed Debenture

3.   First Debenture

4.   Zero Coupon Bond

5.   Zero Interest Bond/Debenture

Features of Debentures

1.   **Maturity period:** Debentures consist of long-term fixed maturity period. Normally, debentures consist of 10–20 years maturity period and are repayable with the principle investment at the end of the maturity period.

2.   **Residual claims in income:** Debenture holders are eligible to get fixed rate of interest at every end of the accounting period. Debenture holders have priority of claim in income of the company over equity and preference shareholders.

3.   **Residual claims on asset:** Debenture holders have

priority of claims on Assets of the company over equity and preference shareholders. The Debenture holders may have either specific change on the Assets or floating change of the assets of the company. Specific change of Debenture holders are treated as secured creditors and floating change of Debenture holders are treated as unsecured creditors.

4.   No voting rights: Debenture holders are considered as creditors of the company. Hence they have no voting rights. Debenture holders cannot have the control over the performance of the business concern.

5.   Fixed rate of interest: Debentures yield fixed rate of interest till the maturity period. Hence the business will not affect the yield of the debenture.

Advantages of Debenture

Debenture is one of the major parts of the long-term sources of finance which of consists the following important advantages:

1.   Long-term sources: Debenture is one of the long-term sources of finance to the company. Normally the maturity period is longer than the other sources of finance.

2.   Fixed rate of interest: Fixed rate of interest is payable to debenture holders, hence it is most suitable of the companies earn higher profit. Generally, the rate of interest is lower than the other sources of long-term finance.

3. **Trade on equity:** A company can trade on equity by mixing debentures in its capital structure and thereby increase its earning per share. When the company apply the trade on equity concept, cost of capital will reduce and value of the company will increase.

4. **Income tax deduction:** Interest payable to debentures can be deducted from the total profit of the company. So it helps to reduce the tax burden of the company.

5. **Protection:** Various provisions of the debenture trust deed and the guidelines issued by the SEB1 protect the interest of debenture holders.

Disadvantages of Debenture

Debenture finance consists of the following major disadvantages:

1.Fixed rate of interest: Debenture consists of fixed rate of interest payable to securities. Even though the company is unable to earn profit, they have to pay the fixed rate of interest to debenture holders, hence, it is not suitable to those company earnings which fluctuate considerably.

2.No voting rights: Debenture holders do not have any

voting rights. Hence, they cannot have the control over the management of the company.

3.Creditors of the company: Debenture holders are merely creditors and not the owners of the company. They do not have any claim in the surplus profits of the company.

4.High risk: Every additional issue of debentures becomes more risky and costly on account of higher expectation of debenture holders. This enhanced financial risk increases the cost of equity capital and the cost of raising finance through debentures which is also high because of high stamp duty.

5.Restrictions of further issues: The company cannot raise further finance through debentures as the debentures are under the part of security of the assets already mortgaged to debenture holders.

INTERNAL FINANCE

A company can mobilize finance through external and internal sources. A new company may not raise internal sources of finance and they can raise finance only external sources such as shares, debentures and loans but an existing company can raise both internal and external sources of finance for their financial requirements. Internal finance is also one of the important sources of finance and it consists of cost of capital while compared to other sources of finance.

Internal source of finance may be broadly classified into two categories:

A. Depreciation Funds

B. Retained earnings

Depreciation Funds

Depreciation funds are the major part of internal sources of finance, which is used to meet the working capital requirements of the business concern. Depreciation means decrease in the value of asset due to wear and tear, lapse of time, obsolescence, exhaustion and accident. Generally depreciation is changed against fixed assets of the company at fixed rate for every year. The purpose of depreciation is replacement of the assets after the expired period. It is one kind of provision of fund, which is needed to reduce the tax burden and overall profitability of the company.

Retained Earnings

Retained earnings are another method of internal sources of finance. Actually is not a method of raising finance, but it is called as accumulation of profits by a company for its expansion and diversification activities.

Retained earnings are called under different names such

as; self finance, inter finance, and plugging back of profits. According to the Companies Act 1956 certain percentage, as prescribed by the central government (not exceeding 10%) of the net profits after tax of a financial year have to be compulsorily transferred to reserve by a company before declaring dividends for the year.

Under the retained earnings sources of finance, a part of the total profits is transferred to various reserves such as general reserve, replacement fund, reserve for repairs and renewals, reserve funds and secrete reserves, etc.

Advantages of Retained Earnings

Retained earnings consist of the following important advantages:

1. **Useful for expansion and diversification**: Retained earnings are most useful to expansion and diversification of the business activities.

2. **Economical sources of finance:** Retained earnings are one of the least costly sources of finance since it does not involve any floatation cost as in the case of raising of funds by issuing different types of securities.

3. **No fixed obligation:** If the companies use equity finance they have to pay dividend and if the companies use debt

finance, they have to pay interest. But if the company uses retained earnings as sources of finance, they need not pay any fixed obligation regarding the payment of dividend or interest.

4.   **Flexible sources:** Retained earnings allow the financial structure to remain completely flexible. The company need not raise loans for further requirements, if it has retained earnings.

5.   **Increase the share value:** When the company uses the retained earnings as the sources of finance for their financial requirements, the cost of capital is very cheaper than the other sources of finance; Hence the value of the share will increase.

6.   **Avoid excessive tax:** Retained earnings provide opportunities for evasion of excessive tax in a company when it has small number of shareholders.

7.   **Increase earning capacity:** Retained earnings consist of least cost of capital and also it is most suitable to those companies which go for diversification and expansion.

Disadvantages of Retained Earnings

Retained earnings also have certain disadvantages:

1.   **Misuses:** The management by manipulating the value of the shares in the stock market can misuse the retained earnings.

2. Leads to monopolies: Excessive use of retained earnings leads to monopolistic attitude of the company.

3. Over capitalization: Retained earnings lead to over capitalization, because if the company uses more and more retained earnings, it leads to insufficient source of finance.

4. Tax evasion: Retained earnings lead to tax evasion. Since, the company reduces tax burden through the retained earnings.

LOAN FINANCING

Loan financing is the important mode of finance raised by the company. Loan finance may be divided into two types:

(a) Long-Term Sources

(b) Short-Term Sources

Financial Institutions

With the effect of the industrial revaluation, the government established nationwide and state wise financial industries to provide long-term financial assistance to industrial concerns in the country. Financial institutions play a key role in the field of industrial development and they are meeting the financial requirements of the business concern. IFCI, ICICI, IDBI, SFC, EXIM Bank, ECGC are the famous financial institutions in the country.

Commercial Banks

Commercial Banks normally provide short-term finance which is repayable within a year. The major finance of commercial banks is as follows:

Short-term advance: Commercial banks provide advance to their customers with or without securities. It is one of the most common and widely used short-term sources of finance, which are needed to meet the working capital requirement of the company.

It is a cheap source of finance, which is in the form of pledge, mortgage, hypothecation and bills discounted and rediscounted.

Short-term Loans

Commercial banks also provide loans to the business concern to meet the short-term financial requirements. When a bank makes an advance in lump sum against some security it is termed as loan. Loan may be in the following form:

(a) **Cash credit**: A cash credit is an arrangement by which a bank allows his customer to borrow money up to certain limit against the security of the commodity.

(b) **Overdraft**: Overdraft is an arrangement with a bank by which a current account holder is allowed to withdraw more than the balance to his credit up to a certain limit without any securities.

Development Banks

Development banks were established mainly for the purpose of promotion and development the industrial sector in the country. Presently, large number of development banks are functioning with multidimensional activities. Development banks are also called as financial institutions or statutory financial institutions or statutory non-banking institutions. Development banks provide two important types of finance:

(a) Direct Finance

(b) Indirect Finance/Refinance

Presently the commercial banks are providing all kinds of financial services including development-banking services. And also nowadays development banks and specialisted financial institutions are providing all kinds of financial services including commercial banking services. Diversified and global financial services are unavoidable to the present day economics. Hence, we can classify the financial institutions only by the structure and set up and not by the services provided by them.

MODEL QUESTIONS

1. Explain the various sources of financing.

2. What is meant by security financing?

3. What is debt financing?

4. Critically examine the advantages and disadvantages of equity shares.

5. Discuss the features of equity shares.

6. What are the merits of the deferred shares?

7. Explain the merits and demerits of preference shares?

8. List out the types of debentures.

Chapter 05

Capital Budgeting

INTRODUCTION

The word Capital refers to be the total investment of a company of firm in money, tangible and intangible assets. Whereas budgeting defined by the **"Rowland** and **William"** it may be said to be the art of building budgets. Budgets are a blue print of a plan and action expressed in quantities and manners.

The examples of capital expenditure:

1. Purchase of fixed assets such as land and building, plant and machinery, good will, etc.

2. The expenditure relating to addition, expansion, improvement and alteration to the fixed assets.

3. The replacement of fixed assets.

4. Research and development project.

[76]

Definitions

According to the definition of **Charles T. Hrongreen,** "capital budgeting is a long-term planning for making and financing proposed capital out lays.

According to the definition of **G.C. Philippatos,** "capital budgeting is concerned with the allocation of the firms source financial resources among the available opportunities. The consideration of investment opportunities involves the comparison of the expected future streams of earnings from a project with the immediate and subsequent streams of earning from a project, with the immediate and subsequent streams of expenditure".

According to the definition of **Richard and Green law,** "capital budgeting is acquiring inputs with long-term return".

According to the definition of **Lyrich,** "capital budgeting consists in planning development of available capital for the purpose of maximizing the long-term profitability of the concern".

It is clearly explained in the above definitions that a firm's scarce financial resources are utilizing the available opportunities. The overall objectives of the company from is to maximize the profits and minimize the expenditure of cost.

Need and Importance of Capital Budgeting

1.   **Huge investments:** Capital budgeting requires huge investments of funds, but the available funds are limited, therefore the firm before investing projects, plan are control its capital expenditure.

2.   **Long-term:** Capital expenditure is long-term in nature or permanent in nature. Therefore financial risks involved in the investment decision are more. If higher risks are involved, it needs careful planning of capital budgeting.

3.   **Irreversible:** The capital investment decisions are irreversible, are not changed back. Once the decision is taken for purchasing a permanent asset, it is very difficult to dispose off those assets without involving huge losses.

4.   **Long-term effect:** Capital budgeting not only reduces the cost but also increases the revenue in long-term and will bring significant changes in the profit of the company by avoiding over or more investment or under investment. Over investments leads to be unable to utilize assets or over utilization of fixed assets. Therefore before making the investment, it is required carefully

planning and analysis of the project thoroughly.

CAPITAL BUDGETING PROCESS

Capital budgeting is a difficult process to the investment of available funds. The benefit will attained only in the near future but, the future is uncertain. However, the following steps followed for capital budgeting, then the process may be easier are.

1. **Identification of various investments proposals:** The capital budgeting may have various investment proposals. The proposal for the investment opportunities may be defined from the top management or may be even from the lower rank. The heads of various department analyse the various investment decisions, and will select proposals submitted to the planning committee of competent authority.

2. **Screening or matching the proposals:** The planning committee will analyse the various proposals and screenings. The selected proposals are considered with the available resources of the concern. Here resources referred as the financial part of the proposal. This reduces the gap between the resources and the investment cost.

3. **Evaluation:** After screening, the proposals are evaluated with the help of various methods, such as pay back period

proposal, net discovered present value method, accounting rate of return and risk analysis. Each method of evaluation used in detail in the later part of this chapter. The proposals are evaluated by.

(a)   Independent proposals

(b)   Contingent of dependent proposals

(c)   Partially exclusive proposals.

Independent proposals are not compared with another proposals and the same may be accepted or rejected. Whereas higher proposals acceptance depends upon the other one or more proposals. For example, the expansion of plant machinery leads to constructing of new building, additional manpower etc. Mutually exclusive projects are those which competed with other proposals and to implement the proposals after considering the risk and return, market demand etc.

4. **Fixing property:** After the evolution, the planning committee will predict which proposals will give more profit or economic consideration. If the projects or proposals are not suitable for the concern's financial condition, the projects are rejected without considering other nature of the proposals.

5. **Final approval:** The planning committee approves the final proposals, with the help of the following:

    (a)   Profitability

    (b)   Economic constituents

    (c)   Financial violability

    (d)   Market conditions.

The planning committee prepares the cost estimation and submits to the management.

6. **Implementing:** The competent autherity spends the money and implements the proposals. While implementing the proposals, assign responsibilities to the proposals, assign responsibilities for completing it, within the time allotted and reduce the cost for this purpose. The network techniques used such as PERT and CPM. It helps the management for monitoring and containing the implementation of the proposals.

7. **Performance review of feedback:** The final stage of capital budgeting is actual results compared with the standard results. The adverse or unfavourable results identified and removing the various difficulties of the project. This is helpful for the future of the proposals.

KINDS OF CAPITAL BUDGETING DECISIONS

[81]

The overall objective of capital budgeting is to maximize the profitability. If a firm concentrates return on investment, this objective can be achieved either by increasing the revenues or reducing the costs. The increasing revenues can be achieved by expansion or the size of operations by adding a new product line. Reducing costs mean representing obsolete return on assets.

METHODS OF CAPITAL BUDGETING OF EVALUATION

By matching the available resources and projects it can be invested. The funds available are always living funds. There are many considerations taken for investment decision process such as environment and economic conditions.

The methods of evaluations are classified as follows:

(A) Traditional methods (or Non-discount methods)

(i)   Pay-back Period Methods

(ii)   Post Pay-back Methods

(iii)   Accounts Rate of Return

(B) Modern methods (or Discount methods)

(i)   Net Present Value Method

(ii)   Internal Rate of Return Method

(iii)   Profitability Index Method

Pay-back Period

Pay-back period is the time required to recover the initial investment in a project.

Merits of Pay-back method

The following are the important merits of the pay-back method:

1. It is easy to calculate and simple to understand.

2. Pay-back method provides further improvement over the accounting rate return.

3. Pay-back method reduces the possibility of loss on account of obsolescence.

Demerits

1. It ignores the time value of money.

2. It ignores all cash inflows after the pay-back period.

3. It is one of the misleading evaluations of capital budgeting.

Accounting Rate of Return or Average Rate of Return

Average rate of return means the average rate of return or profit taken for considering the project evaluation. This method is one of the traditional methods for evaluating the project proposals:

Merits

1. It is easy to calculate and simple to understand.

2. It is based on the accounting information rather than cash inflow.

3. It is not based on the time value of money.

4. It considers the total benefits associated with the project.

Demerits

1. It ignores the time value of money.

2. It ignores the reinvestment potential of a project.

3. Different methods are used for accounting profit. So, it leads to some difficulties in the calculation of the project.

Net Present Value

Net present value method is one of the modern methods for evaluating the project proposals. In this method cash inflows are considered with the time value of the money. Net present value describes as the summation of the present value of cash inflow and present value of cash outflow. Net present value is the difference between the total present value of future cash inflows and the total present value of future cash outflows.

Merits

1. It recognizes the time value of money.

2. It considers the total benefits arising out of the proposal.

3. It is the best method for the selection of mutually exclusive projects.

4. It helps to achieve the maximization of shareholders' wealth.

Demerits

1. It is difficult to understand and calculate.

2. It needs the discount factors for calculation of present values.

3. It is not suitable for the projects having different effective lives.

4. Internal Rate of Return

5. Internal rate of return is time adjusted technique and covers the disadvantages of the traditional techniques. In other words it is a rate at which discount cash flows to zero. It is expected by the following ratio:

Merits

1. It consider the time value of money.

2. It takes into account the total cash inflow and outflow.

3. It does not use the concept of the required rate of return.

4. It gives the approximate/nearest rate of return.

Demerits

1. It involves complicated computational method.

2. It produces multiple rates which may be confusing for taking decisions.

3. It is assume that all intermediate cash flows are reinvested at the internal rate of return.

RISK AND UNCERTAINLY IN CAPITAL BUDGETING

Capital budgeting requires the projection of cash inflow and outflow of the future. The future in always uncertain, estimate of demand, production, selling price, cost etc., cannot be exact.

For example: The product at any time it become obsolete therefore, the future in unexpected. The following methods for considering the accounting of risk in capital budgeting. Various evaluation methods are used for risk and uncertainty in capital budgeting are as follows:

(i) Risk-adjusted cut off rate (or method of varying discount rate)

(ii) Certainly equivalent method.

(iii) Sensitivity technique.

(iv) Probability technique

(v) Standard deviation method.

(vi) Co-efficient of variation method.

(vii) Decision tree analysis.